50 Wild and Forged Recipes for Home

By: Kelly Johnson

Table of Contents

- Wild Mushroom Risotto
- Dandelion Greens Salad
- Nettle Soup
- Acorn Flour Pancakes
- Elderflower Cordial
- Wild Berry Jam
- Ramp Pesto
- Fiddlehead Fern Frittata
- Garlic Mustard Stir-Fry
- Wild Duck Confit
- Birch Syrup Glazed Carrots
- Foraged Greens Quiche
- Purslane Salad
- Seaweed Salad
- Chanterelle Mushroom Pasta
- Wildflower Honey Granola
- Sunchoke Hash
- Wild Rice Pilaf
- Blueberry Buckle
- Acorn Bread
- Cedar Plank Salmon
- Wild Herb Chimichurri
- Crabapple Jelly
- Roasted Beet and Foraged Greens Salad
- Wild Game Stew
- Spruce Tip Infused Syrup
- Blackberry Crisp
- Wood Sorrel Soup
- Stinging Nettle Tea
- Pine Needle Tea
- Foraged Fruit Sorbet
- Chive Blossom Vinegar
- Herbal Infused Oil
- Wild Apple Chutney
- Sweet Potato and Wild Greens Casserole

- Ramps and Bacon Quiche
- Lamb's Quarters Tacos
- Wild Asparagus Tart
- Maple-Glazed Roasted Vegetables
- Ginger and Wild Mint Tea
- Fennel and Wild Herb Sausage
- Hawthorn Berry Ketchup
- Ground Cherry Pie
- Elderberry Syrup
- Foraged Salad Rolls
- Wild Garlic Butter
- Rose Hip Jam
- Savory Mushroom Galette
- Wild Cherry Clafoutis
- Dandelion Wine

Wild Mushroom Risotto

Ingredients:

- 1 cup Arborio rice
- 4 cups vegetable broth
- 1 cup wild mushrooms, chopped
- 1 onion, chopped
- 2 cloves garlic, minced
- 1/2 cup white wine (optional)
- 1/2 cup Parmesan cheese, grated
- 2 tablespoons olive oil
- Salt and pepper (to taste)
- Fresh herbs (for garnish)

Instructions:

1. **Prepare Broth**: In a saucepan, heat vegetable broth and keep warm.
2. **Sauté Onions and Garlic**: In a large skillet, heat olive oil over medium heat. Add onion and garlic, sauté until translucent.
3. **Cook Mushrooms**: Add wild mushrooms and cook until softened.
4. **Add Rice**: Stir in Arborio rice and cook for 1-2 minutes. If using, pour in white wine and stir until absorbed.
5. **Add Broth Gradually**: Add warm broth one ladle at a time, stirring frequently until absorbed before adding more. Continue until rice is creamy and al dente, about 18-20 minutes.
6. **Finish**: Stir in Parmesan cheese, salt, and pepper. Garnish with fresh herbs before serving.

Dandelion Greens Salad

Ingredients:

- 4 cups dandelion greens, washed and torn
- 1/2 cup cherry tomatoes, halved
- 1/4 cup red onion, thinly sliced
- 1/4 cup feta cheese, crumbled
- 1/4 cup olive oil
- 2 tablespoons balsamic vinegar
- Salt and pepper (to taste)

Instructions:

1. **Prepare Dressing**: In a small bowl, whisk together olive oil, balsamic vinegar, salt, and pepper.
2. **Combine Ingredients**: In a large bowl, toss dandelion greens, cherry tomatoes, red onion, and feta cheese.
3. **Dress Salad**: Drizzle the dressing over the salad and toss gently. Serve immediately.

Nettle Soup

Ingredients:

- 4 cups fresh nettles, stems removed
- 1 onion, chopped
- 2 cloves garlic, minced
- 4 cups vegetable broth
- 1 potato, peeled and diced
- 2 tablespoons olive oil
- Salt and pepper (to taste)
- Cream (for garnish, optional)

Instructions:

1. **Sauté Onions and Garlic**: In a pot, heat olive oil over medium heat. Add onion and garlic, sauté until translucent.
2. **Add Potatoes**: Stir in diced potato and cook for a few minutes.
3. **Add Broth and Nettles**: Pour in vegetable broth and bring to a boil. Add nettles and cook until tender, about 10 minutes.
4. **Blend**: Use an immersion blender to puree the soup until smooth. Season with salt and pepper. Serve warm, garnished with a drizzle of cream if desired.

Acorn Flour Pancakes

Ingredients:

- 1 cup acorn flour
- 1/2 cup all-purpose flour
- 2 tablespoons sugar
- 1 tablespoon baking powder
- 1/2 teaspoon salt
- 1 cup milk
- 2 eggs
- 2 tablespoons melted butter

Instructions:

1. **Mix Dry Ingredients**: In a bowl, combine acorn flour, all-purpose flour, sugar, baking powder, and salt.
2. **Combine Wet Ingredients**: In another bowl, whisk together milk, eggs, and melted butter.
3. **Combine Mixtures**: Pour wet ingredients into dry ingredients and stir until just combined.
4. **Cook Pancakes**: Heat a griddle over medium heat. Pour batter to form pancakes and cook until bubbles form, then flip and cook until golden brown. Serve warm with syrup.

Elderflower Cordial

Ingredients:

- 20 elderflower heads
- 4 cups water
- 2 cups sugar
- 1 lemon, sliced
- 1 tablespoon citric acid (optional)

Instructions:

1. **Make Syrup**: In a saucepan, bring water and sugar to a boil, stirring until sugar dissolves.
2. **Add Ingredients**: Remove from heat and add elderflower heads, lemon slices, and citric acid. Cover and let steep for 24 hours.
3. **Strain**: Strain the mixture through a fine sieve into bottles. Store in the refrigerator. Dilute with water or sparkling water to serve.

Wild Berry Jam

Ingredients:

- 4 cups mixed wild berries (e.g., blackberries, raspberries, blueberries)
- 1 cup sugar
- 2 tablespoons lemon juice
- 1 tablespoon pectin (optional, for thicker jam)

Instructions:

1. **Cook Berries**: In a saucepan, combine wild berries, sugar, and lemon juice. Cook over medium heat, stirring until berries break down.
2. **Add Pectin**: If using, stir in pectin and boil for 1-2 minutes.
3. **Test Consistency**: To test, spoon a little jam onto a plate; if it sets, it's ready.
4. **Jar Jam**: Pour into sterilized jars and let cool. Store in the refrigerator.

Ramp Pesto

Ingredients:

- 1 cup ramps, cleaned and chopped (bulbs and leaves)
- 1/2 cup nuts (pine nuts or walnuts)
- 1/2 cup Parmesan cheese, grated
- 1/2 cup olive oil
- Salt and pepper (to taste)

Instructions:

1. **Blend Ingredients**: In a food processor, combine ramps, nuts, Parmesan, salt, and pepper. Pulse until finely chopped.
2. **Add Olive Oil**: With the processor running, slowly add olive oil until the mixture is smooth. Adjust seasoning to taste.
3. **Serve**: Use immediately with pasta, on sandwiches, or as a dip.

Fiddlehead Fern Frittata

Ingredients:

- 1 cup fiddlehead ferns, cleaned
- 6 eggs
- 1/2 cup milk
- 1/2 cup cheese (cheddar or feta), crumbled
- 1 onion, chopped
- 2 tablespoons olive oil
- Salt and pepper (to taste)

Instructions:

1. **Preheat Oven**: Preheat the oven to 350°F (175°C).
2. **Sauté Onions and Fiddleheads**: In an oven-safe skillet, heat olive oil over medium heat. Add onion and fiddleheads, sauté for about 5 minutes until tender.
3. **Whisk Eggs**: In a bowl, whisk together eggs, milk, cheese, salt, and pepper. Pour over the sautéed vegetables.
4. **Cook and Bake**: Cook on the stovetop until edges set, then transfer to the oven and bake for 15-20 minutes until fully set. Slice and serve warm.

Enjoy these delicious and foraged-inspired dishes!

Garlic Mustard Stir-Fry

Ingredients:

- 2 cups garlic mustard greens, chopped
- 1 bell pepper, sliced
- 1 onion, sliced
- 2 cloves garlic, minced
- 2 tablespoons soy sauce
- 1 tablespoon olive oil
- Salt and pepper (to taste)
- Sesame seeds (for garnish)

Instructions:

1. **Heat Oil**: In a large skillet, heat olive oil over medium heat.
2. **Sauté Vegetables**: Add onion and bell pepper, and sauté until softened. Add garlic and cook for an additional minute.
3. **Add Greens**: Stir in garlic mustard greens and cook until wilted, about 3-4 minutes.
4. **Season**: Add soy sauce, salt, and pepper. Toss to combine and cook for another minute.
5. **Serve**: Garnish with sesame seeds and serve warm.

Wild Duck Confit

Ingredients:

- 4 duck legs
- 4 cups duck fat (or enough to cover the legs)
- 2 cloves garlic, smashed
- 2 sprigs fresh thyme
- Salt and pepper (to taste)

Instructions:

1. **Season Duck**: Generously season duck legs with salt and pepper. Place in a bowl with garlic and thyme, cover, and refrigerate overnight.
2. **Preheat Oven**: Preheat the oven to 225°F (110°C).
3. **Cook Duck**: In a deep baking dish, cover the duck legs with duck fat. Cook in the oven for 4-5 hours until tender.
4. **Cool and Store**: Let cool in the fat. Store in the refrigerator, ensuring the legs are covered with fat for preservation.

Birch Syrup Glazed Carrots

Ingredients:

- 1 lb carrots, peeled and sliced
- 1/4 cup birch syrup
- 2 tablespoons butter
- Salt and pepper (to taste)
- Fresh parsley (for garnish)

Instructions:

1. **Cook Carrots**: In a pot of boiling salted water, cook carrots until tender, about 5-7 minutes. Drain.
2. **Glaze**: In a skillet, melt butter and add birch syrup. Stir in cooked carrots, tossing to coat.
3. **Season**: Cook for a few minutes until the glaze thickens slightly. Season with salt and pepper.
4. **Serve**: Garnish with fresh parsley and serve warm.

Foraged Greens Quiche

Ingredients:

- 1 pie crust (store-bought or homemade)
- 2 cups mixed foraged greens (e.g., nettles, dandelion greens, garlic mustard)
- 4 large eggs
- 1 cup heavy cream
- 1 cup cheese (gruyère or feta), crumbled
- Salt and pepper (to taste)

Instructions:

1. **Preheat Oven**: Preheat the oven to 375°F (190°C).
2. **Prepare Greens**: Sauté foraged greens in a pan until wilted. Set aside.
3. **Mix Filling**: In a bowl, whisk together eggs, cream, salt, and pepper. Stir in sautéed greens and cheese.
4. **Assemble Quiche**: Pour filling into the pie crust. Bake for 30-35 minutes until set and golden.
5. **Cool and Serve**: Let cool for a few minutes before slicing. Serve warm.

Purslane Salad

Ingredients:

- 2 cups fresh purslane, rinsed and chopped
- 1 cucumber, diced
- 1 cup cherry tomatoes, halved
- 1/4 red onion, thinly sliced
- 2 tablespoons olive oil
- 1 tablespoon lemon juice
- Salt and pepper (to taste)

Instructions:

1. **Combine Ingredients**: In a large bowl, combine purslane, cucumber, tomatoes, and red onion.
2. **Make Dressing**: In a small bowl, whisk together olive oil, lemon juice, salt, and pepper.
3. **Dress Salad**: Drizzle the dressing over the salad and toss gently. Serve immediately.

Seaweed Salad

Ingredients:

- 1 cup dried seaweed (wakame or similar), rehydrated
- 1/4 cucumber, julienned
- 1 carrot, julienned
- 2 tablespoons rice vinegar
- 1 tablespoon soy sauce
- 1 teaspoon sesame oil
- Sesame seeds (for garnish)

Instructions:

1. **Prepare Seaweed**: Rehydrate the dried seaweed according to package instructions. Drain and squeeze out excess water.
2. **Combine Vegetables**: In a bowl, mix rehydrated seaweed, cucumber, and carrot.
3. **Make Dressing**: In a small bowl, whisk together rice vinegar, soy sauce, and sesame oil.
4. **Dress Salad**: Pour the dressing over the salad and toss to combine. Garnish with sesame seeds and serve chilled.

Chanterelle Mushroom Pasta

Ingredients:

- 8 oz pasta of choice
- 2 cups chanterelle mushrooms, cleaned and sliced
- 2 cloves garlic, minced
- 1/2 cup heavy cream
- 1/4 cup Parmesan cheese, grated
- 2 tablespoons olive oil
- Salt and pepper (to taste)
- Fresh parsley (for garnish)

Instructions:

1. **Cook Pasta**: Cook pasta according to package instructions. Drain and set aside.
2. **Sauté Mushrooms**: In a skillet, heat olive oil over medium heat. Add garlic and chanterelle mushrooms; sauté until golden.
3. **Make Sauce**: Stir in heavy cream and Parmesan cheese. Cook until thickened slightly. Season with salt and pepper.
4. **Combine**: Toss cooked pasta with the mushroom sauce. Serve garnished with fresh parsley.

Wildflower Honey Granola

Ingredients:

- 2 cups rolled oats
- 1 cup nuts (almonds, walnuts, etc.), chopped
- 1/2 cup seeds (pumpkin or sunflower)
- 1/2 cup wildflower honey
- 1/4 cup vegetable oil
- 1 teaspoon vanilla extract
- 1/2 teaspoon salt
- Optional: dried fruits (raisins, cranberries) for serving

Instructions:

1. **Preheat Oven**: Preheat the oven to 350°F (175°C).
2. **Mix Ingredients**: In a large bowl, combine oats, nuts, seeds, honey, oil, vanilla, and salt. Mix well.
3. **Bake**: Spread the mixture on a baking sheet and bake for 20-25 minutes, stirring halfway through, until golden.
4. **Cool and Store**: Let cool completely before storing in an airtight container. Serve with yogurt or milk, adding dried fruits if desired.

Enjoy these foraged and delicious dishes!

Sunchoke Hash

Ingredients:

- 2 cups sunchokes, peeled and diced
- 1 onion, chopped
- 1 bell pepper, diced
- 2 cloves garlic, minced
- 2 tablespoons olive oil
- Salt and pepper (to taste)
- Fresh herbs (for garnish)

Instructions:

1. **Heat Oil**: In a skillet, heat olive oil over medium heat.
2. **Sauté Vegetables**: Add onion and bell pepper, cooking until softened. Stir in garlic and cook for another minute.
3. **Add Sunchokes**: Add diced sunchokes, season with salt and pepper, and cook until golden and tender, about 10-15 minutes.
4. **Serve**: Garnish with fresh herbs and serve warm.

Wild Rice Pilaf

Ingredients:

- 1 cup wild rice
- 2 cups vegetable broth
- 1 onion, chopped
- 1/2 cup celery, diced
- 1/2 cup carrots, diced
- 2 tablespoons olive oil
- Salt and pepper (to taste)
- Fresh parsley (for garnish)

Instructions:

1. **Sauté Vegetables**: In a pot, heat olive oil over medium heat. Add onion, celery, and carrots, sautéing until softened.
2. **Add Rice and Broth**: Stir in wild rice and vegetable broth. Bring to a boil, then reduce heat to low. Cover and simmer for 45-50 minutes, or until rice is tender.
3. **Fluff and Serve**: Remove from heat, fluff with a fork, and season with salt and pepper. Garnish with fresh parsley before serving.

Blueberry Buckle

Ingredients:

- 2 cups fresh blueberries
- 1 1/2 cups all-purpose flour
- 1 teaspoon baking powder
- 1/2 teaspoon salt
- 1/2 cup butter, softened
- 1 cup sugar
- 2 large eggs
- 1 teaspoon vanilla extract
- 1/2 cup milk
- 1/2 teaspoon cinnamon (for topping)

Instructions:

1. **Preheat Oven**: Preheat the oven to 350°F (175°C). Grease a 9-inch square baking dish.
2. **Mix Dry Ingredients**: In a bowl, whisk together flour, baking powder, and salt.
3. **Cream Butter and Sugar**: In another bowl, cream together butter and sugar until light. Beat in eggs and vanilla.
4. **Combine Mixtures**: Gradually add dry ingredients to the butter mixture, alternating with milk. Fold in blueberries.
5. **Bake**: Pour into the prepared dish and sprinkle with cinnamon. Bake for 40-45 minutes or until golden and a toothpick comes out clean. Let cool before serving.

Acorn Bread

Ingredients:

- 1 cup acorn flour
- 1 cup all-purpose flour
- 1 tablespoon baking powder
- 1/2 teaspoon salt
- 1 cup milk
- 1/4 cup honey
- 1/4 cup melted butter
- 2 large eggs

Instructions:

1. **Preheat Oven**: Preheat the oven to 350°F (175°C). Grease a loaf pan.
2. **Mix Dry Ingredients**: In a bowl, combine acorn flour, all-purpose flour, baking powder, and salt.
3. **Combine Wet Ingredients**: In another bowl, whisk together milk, honey, melted butter, and eggs.
4. **Combine Mixtures**: Add wet ingredients to dry ingredients and stir until just combined. Pour into the prepared loaf pan.
5. **Bake**: Bake for 40-45 minutes until a toothpick inserted comes out clean. Let cool before slicing.

Cedar Plank Salmon

Ingredients:

- 1 salmon fillet (about 1 lb)
- 1 cedar plank (soaked in water for at least 1 hour)
- 2 tablespoons olive oil
- 2 tablespoons lemon juice
- Salt and pepper (to taste)
- Fresh herbs (dill or parsley, for garnish)

Instructions:

1. **Preheat Grill**: Preheat the grill to medium heat.
2. **Prepare Salmon**: Rub salmon with olive oil, lemon juice, salt, and pepper.
3. **Grill on Cedar Plank**: Place the soaked cedar plank on the grill. Once it begins to smoke, place the salmon on the plank. Close the lid and grill for about 15-20 minutes, or until the salmon is cooked through.
4. **Serve**: Garnish with fresh herbs and serve directly from the plank.

Wild Herb Chimichurri

Ingredients:

- 1 cup fresh herbs (parsley, cilantro, or a mix)
- 2 cloves garlic, minced
- 1/2 cup olive oil
- 1/4 cup vinegar (red wine or apple cider)
- 1 teaspoon red pepper flakes
- Salt and pepper (to taste)

Instructions:

1. **Combine Ingredients**: In a bowl, mix chopped herbs, garlic, olive oil, vinegar, red pepper flakes, salt, and pepper.
2. **Blend (optional)**: For a smoother texture, blend in a food processor.
3. **Serve**: Use as a sauce for grilled meats or vegetables.

Crabapple Jelly

Ingredients:

- 4 cups crabapple juice
- 1/4 cup lemon juice
- 1 package (1.75 oz) pectin
- 5 cups sugar

Instructions:

1. **Prepare Juice**: Extract juice from crabapples by simmering them in water, then straining.
2. **Cook Mixture**: In a pot, combine crabapple juice, lemon juice, and pectin. Bring to a boil.
3. **Add Sugar**: Stir in sugar and bring back to a boil, cooking for 1-2 minutes.
4. **Jar Jelly**: Pour into sterilized jars and seal. Let cool completely before storing.

Roasted Beet and Foraged Greens Salad

Ingredients:

- 2 medium beets, roasted and diced
- 2 cups foraged greens (e.g., dandelion, arugula)
- 1/4 cup goat cheese, crumbled
- 1/4 cup walnuts, toasted
- 2 tablespoons balsamic vinegar
- 2 tablespoons olive oil
- Salt and pepper (to taste)

Instructions:

1. **Roast Beets**: Preheat the oven to 400°F (200°C). Wrap beets in foil and roast for 45-60 minutes until tender. Let cool, peel, and dice.
2. **Combine Salad**: In a large bowl, combine roasted beets, foraged greens, goat cheese, and walnuts.
3. **Dress Salad**: In a small bowl, whisk together balsamic vinegar, olive oil, salt, and pepper. Drizzle over the salad and toss gently.
4. **Serve**: Serve immediately, garnished with additional cheese and nuts if desired.

Enjoy these delightful dishes inspired by foraged and seasonal ingredients!

Wild Game Stew

Ingredients:

- 2 lbs wild game meat (venison, elk, or rabbit), cut into chunks
- 2 tablespoons olive oil
- 1 onion, chopped
- 2 carrots, diced
- 2 celery stalks, diced
- 3 cloves garlic, minced
- 4 cups beef or vegetable broth
- 2 cups potatoes, diced
- 1 teaspoon dried thyme
- 1 teaspoon rosemary
- Salt and pepper (to taste)
- Fresh parsley (for garnish)

Instructions:

1. **Brown Meat**: In a large pot, heat olive oil over medium-high heat. Brown the wild game meat on all sides, then remove and set aside.
2. **Sauté Vegetables**: In the same pot, add onion, carrots, and celery. Cook until softened, about 5-7 minutes. Stir in garlic and cook for another minute.
3. **Combine Ingredients**: Return the meat to the pot. Add broth, potatoes, thyme, rosemary, salt, and pepper. Bring to a boil.
4. **Simmer**: Reduce heat to low, cover, and simmer for 1.5 to 2 hours, or until the meat is tender.
5. **Serve**: Garnish with fresh parsley and serve warm.

Spruce Tip Infused Syrup

Ingredients:

- 1 cup spruce tips, fresh and young
- 1 cup sugar
- 1 cup water

Instructions:

1. **Combine Ingredients**: In a saucepan, combine spruce tips, sugar, and water.
2. **Heat Mixture**: Bring to a gentle boil, stirring until the sugar dissolves.
3. **Steep**: Remove from heat and let steep for 30 minutes. Strain the mixture into a clean jar.
4. **Store**: Let cool before sealing. Use as a syrup for pancakes, waffles, or cocktails.

Blackberry Crisp

Ingredients:

- 4 cups fresh blackberries
- 1/2 cup sugar
- 1 tablespoon cornstarch
- 1 teaspoon lemon juice
- 1 cup rolled oats
- 1/2 cup flour
- 1/2 cup brown sugar
- 1/2 teaspoon cinnamon
- 1/4 cup butter, melted

Instructions:

1. **Preheat Oven**: Preheat the oven to 350°F (175°C).
2. **Prepare Filling**: In a bowl, combine blackberries, sugar, cornstarch, and lemon juice. Transfer to a greased baking dish.
3. **Make Topping**: In another bowl, mix oats, flour, brown sugar, cinnamon, and melted butter until crumbly.
4. **Assemble and Bake**: Sprinkle the topping over the blackberry mixture. Bake for 30-35 minutes until bubbly and golden.
5. **Serve**: Let cool slightly and serve warm, optionally with ice cream.

Wood Sorrel Soup

Ingredients:

- 4 cups fresh wood sorrel, rinsed and chopped
- 1 onion, chopped
- 2 cloves garlic, minced
- 4 cups vegetable broth
- 1 potato, peeled and diced
- 1 tablespoon olive oil
- Salt and pepper (to taste)
- Cream (for serving, optional)

Instructions:

1. **Sauté Onion and Garlic**: In a pot, heat olive oil over medium heat. Add onion and garlic, cooking until softened.
2. **Add Broth and Potatoes**: Stir in the vegetable broth and potatoes. Bring to a boil, then simmer until the potatoes are tender, about 15 minutes.
3. **Add Wood Sorrel**: Stir in the chopped wood sorrel and cook for another 5 minutes.
4. **Blend Soup**: Use an immersion blender to puree the soup until smooth. Season with salt and pepper.
5. **Serve**: Ladle into bowls, drizzling with cream if desired.

Stinging Nettle Tea

Ingredients:

- 1 cup fresh stinging nettles, rinsed (or 1 tablespoon dried nettles)
- 4 cups water
- Honey or lemon (for serving, optional)

Instructions:

1. **Boil Water**: Bring water to a boil in a pot.
2. **Steep Nettle**: Add stinging nettles to the boiling water. Remove from heat and let steep for 10-15 minutes.
3. **Strain and Serve**: Strain the tea into cups. Sweeten with honey or lemon if desired.

Pine Needle Tea

Ingredients:

- 1 cup fresh pine needles, rinsed (ensure they are from a safe species)
- 4 cups water
- Honey or lemon (for serving, optional)

Instructions:

1. **Boil Water**: Bring water to a boil in a pot.
2. **Steep Pine Needles**: Add pine needles to the boiling water. Remove from heat and let steep for 10-15 minutes.
3. **Strain and Serve**: Strain the tea into cups. Sweeten with honey or lemon if desired.

Foraged Fruit Sorbet

Ingredients:

- 2 cups foraged fruits (such as wild blackberries, raspberries, or blueberries)
- 1/2 cup sugar
- 1 tablespoon lemon juice
- 1/2 cup water

Instructions:

1. **Make Syrup**: In a saucepan, combine sugar and water. Heat until sugar dissolves, then let cool.
2. **Blend Fruits**: In a blender, combine foraged fruits, syrup, and lemon juice. Blend until smooth.
3. **Freeze**: Pour the mixture into a shallow dish and freeze for at least 4 hours, stirring every hour until it reaches a sorbet consistency.
4. **Serve**: Scoop into bowls and enjoy!

Chive Blossom Vinegar

Ingredients:

- 1 cup chive blossoms
- 2 cups white wine vinegar

Instructions:

1. **Prepare Blossoms**: Gently rinse chive blossoms and pack them into a clean jar.
2. **Add Vinegar**: Pour white wine vinegar over the blossoms, ensuring they are fully submerged.
3. **Infuse**: Seal the jar and let it sit in a cool, dark place for 2-4 weeks, shaking occasionally.
4. **Strain and Store**: Strain the vinegar into a clean bottle. Use it in dressings or marinades.

Enjoy these unique and flavorful recipes inspired by nature!

Herbal Infused Oil

Ingredients:

- 1 cup olive oil
- 1/2 cup fresh herbs (such as rosemary, thyme, or basil)
- Optional: garlic cloves, chili flakes

Instructions:

1. **Combine Ingredients**: In a saucepan, combine olive oil and herbs (and any optional ingredients).
2. **Heat Gently**: Heat over low heat for about 30 minutes, ensuring the oil doesn't boil.
3. **Cool and Strain**: Let the oil cool, then strain into a clean bottle.
4. **Store**: Seal and store in a cool, dark place. Use for drizzling over dishes or in dressings.

Wild Apple Chutney

Ingredients:

- 4 cups wild apples, peeled and chopped
- 1 cup onion, chopped
- 1 cup brown sugar
- 1/2 cup apple cider vinegar
- 1 teaspoon cinnamon
- 1/2 teaspoon nutmeg
- Salt (to taste)

Instructions:

1. **Combine Ingredients**: In a large pot, combine all ingredients.
2. **Cook Mixture**: Bring to a boil, then reduce heat and simmer for about 30-40 minutes, stirring occasionally, until thickened.
3. **Cool and Store**: Let cool and transfer to jars. Store in the refrigerator for up to a month.

Sweet Potato and Wild Greens Casserole

Ingredients:

- 2 large sweet potatoes, peeled and sliced
- 2 cups wild greens (like dandelion or lamb's quarters), chopped
- 1 cup ricotta cheese
- 1/2 cup grated cheese (cheddar or mozzarella)
- 2 eggs
- Salt and pepper (to taste)

Instructions:

1. **Preheat Oven**: Preheat the oven to 375°F (190°C).
2. **Prepare Mixture**: In a bowl, mix ricotta, eggs, wild greens, salt, and pepper.
3. **Layer Casserole**: In a greased baking dish, layer sweet potato slices and the ricotta mixture, repeating layers.
4. **Top with Cheese**: Sprinkle grated cheese on top.
5. **Bake**: Cover with foil and bake for 30 minutes. Remove foil and bake for an additional 15 minutes, until golden and bubbly.

Ramps and Bacon Quiche

Ingredients:

- 1 pie crust (store-bought or homemade)
- 1 cup ramps, cleaned and chopped
- 4 slices bacon, cooked and crumbled
- 4 eggs
- 1 cup heavy cream
- Salt and pepper (to taste)
- 1 cup shredded cheese (cheddar or Swiss)

Instructions:

1. **Preheat Oven**: Preheat the oven to 375°F (190°C).
2. **Cook Ramps**: Sauté ramps in a skillet until tender, about 5 minutes.
3. **Whisk Eggs and Cream**: In a bowl, whisk together eggs, cream, salt, and pepper.
4. **Assemble Quiche**: Place ramps and bacon in the pie crust. Pour egg mixture over and top with cheese.
5. **Bake**: Bake for 35-40 minutes until set and golden. Let cool slightly before slicing.

Lamb's Quarters Tacos

Ingredients:

- 2 cups lamb's quarters, chopped
- 1 cup black beans (cooked or canned)
- 1 teaspoon cumin
- 1 teaspoon chili powder
- Corn tortillas
- Toppings: avocado, salsa, cheese, cilantro

Instructions:

1. **Sauté Greens**: In a skillet, sauté lamb's quarters until wilted, about 3-4 minutes. Add black beans, cumin, and chili powder. Cook for another 2-3 minutes.
2. **Warm Tortillas**: Heat corn tortillas in a separate skillet until pliable.
3. **Assemble Tacos**: Spoon the lamb's quarters mixture onto tortillas and add desired toppings.
4. **Serve**: Serve warm and enjoy!

Wild Asparagus Tart

Ingredients:

- 1 sheet puff pastry, thawed
- 1 cup wild asparagus, trimmed
- 1 cup ricotta cheese
- 1 egg
- Salt and pepper (to taste)
- Grated cheese (Parmesan or feta)

Instructions:

1. **Preheat Oven**: Preheat the oven to 400°F (200°C).
2. **Prepare Pastry**: Roll out puff pastry and place it on a baking sheet lined with parchment paper. Score a border around the edge.
3. **Mix Filling**: In a bowl, mix ricotta, egg, salt, and pepper.
4. **Assemble Tart**: Spread ricotta mixture on the pastry and top with wild asparagus and grated cheese.
5. **Bake**: Bake for 25-30 minutes until golden and puffed. Let cool slightly before slicing.

Maple-Glazed Roasted Vegetables

Ingredients:

- 4 cups mixed vegetables (carrots, Brussels sprouts, sweet potatoes, etc.), chopped
- 2 tablespoons olive oil
- 2 tablespoons maple syrup
- Salt and pepper (to taste)

Instructions:

1. **Preheat Oven**: Preheat the oven to 425°F (220°C).
2. **Toss Vegetables**: In a bowl, toss vegetables with olive oil, maple syrup, salt, and pepper.
3. **Roast**: Spread on a baking sheet in a single layer. Roast for 25-30 minutes until tender and caramelized.
4. **Serve**: Serve warm as a side dish.

Ginger and Wild Mint Tea

Ingredients:

- 1 cup fresh ginger, sliced
- 1 cup fresh wild mint leaves
- 4 cups water
- Honey or lemon (for serving, optional)

Instructions:

1. **Boil Water**: Bring water to a boil in a pot.
2. **Add Ingredients**: Add sliced ginger and mint leaves to the boiling water. Reduce heat and let simmer for 10-15 minutes.
3. **Strain and Serve**: Strain the tea into cups. Sweeten with honey or lemon if desired.

Enjoy these delightful recipes that celebrate the flavors of foraged and seasonal ingredients!

Fennel and Wild Herb Sausage

Ingredients:

- 1 lb ground pork (or any preferred meat)
- 1 tablespoon fennel seeds, crushed
- 1/4 cup fresh wild herbs (like parsley, thyme, or oregano), chopped
- 2 cloves garlic, minced
- 1 teaspoon salt
- 1/2 teaspoon black pepper
- 1/2 teaspoon red pepper flakes (optional)
- Sausage casings (optional)

Instructions:

1. **Mix Ingredients**: In a bowl, combine ground meat, fennel seeds, wild herbs, garlic, salt, pepper, and red pepper flakes. Mix well.
2. **Stuff Sausages (optional)**: If using casings, stuff the mixture into sausage casings and tie off the ends. If not, form into patties or meatballs.
3. **Cook**: Grill or pan-fry the sausages over medium heat until cooked through, about 6-8 minutes per side.
4. **Serve**: Enjoy on their own or in a sandwich.

Hawthorn Berry Ketchup

Ingredients:

- 2 cups hawthorn berries, rinsed
- 1 cup apple cider vinegar
- 1/2 cup brown sugar
- 1/2 cup onion, chopped
- 1 clove garlic, minced
- 1 teaspoon salt
- 1/2 teaspoon cinnamon
- 1/2 teaspoon allspice

Instructions:

1. **Cook Berries**: In a saucepan, combine hawthorn berries, vinegar, brown sugar, onion, garlic, salt, cinnamon, and allspice. Bring to a boil.
2. **Simmer**: Reduce heat and simmer for about 30 minutes, until berries are soft.
3. **Blend**: Use an immersion blender or regular blender to puree the mixture until smooth.
4. **Strain**: Strain through a fine mesh sieve if desired for a smoother texture. Store in sterilized jars in the refrigerator.

Ground Cherry Pie

Ingredients:

- 2 cups ground cherries, husked and rinsed
- 1 cup sugar
- 1 tablespoon cornstarch
- 1 tablespoon lemon juice
- 1 teaspoon vanilla extract
- 1 pie crust (store-bought or homemade)

Instructions:

1. **Preheat Oven**: Preheat the oven to 375°F (190°C).
2. **Prepare Filling**: In a bowl, mix ground cherries, sugar, cornstarch, lemon juice, and vanilla until combined.
3. **Assemble Pie**: Pour the filling into the pie crust and cover with a top crust, sealing the edges.
4. **Bake**: Cut slits in the top crust for steam to escape. Bake for 30-35 minutes, until golden brown and bubbly.
5. **Cool**: Let cool before slicing and serving.

Elderberry Syrup

Ingredients:

- 1 cup dried elderberries
- 4 cups water
- 1 cup honey (or to taste)
- 1 tablespoon lemon juice

Instructions:

1. **Boil Ingredients**: In a saucepan, combine elderberries and water. Bring to a boil, then reduce heat and simmer for 30-40 minutes.
2. **Strain**: Remove from heat and strain the liquid through a fine mesh sieve, discarding the solids.
3. **Sweeten**: Stir in honey and lemon juice until dissolved. Let cool before transferring to a bottle.
4. **Store**: Refrigerate and use as a natural remedy or flavoring.

Foraged Salad Rolls

Ingredients:

- Rice paper wrappers
- Mixed foraged greens (like dandelion, lamb's quarters, or wild mint)
- Sliced vegetables (carrots, cucumbers, radishes)
- Cooked protein (shrimp, chicken, or tofu)
- Dipping sauce (peanut sauce or soy sauce)

Instructions:

1. **Prepare Fillings**: Gather foraged greens, sliced vegetables, and protein.
2. **Soak Wrappers**: Soak rice paper wrappers in warm water until pliable.
3. **Assemble Rolls**: Lay the soaked wrapper on a clean surface. Add a small amount of each filling, folding in the sides and rolling tightly.
4. **Serve**: Serve with dipping sauce on the side.

Wild Garlic Butter

Ingredients:

- 1 cup unsalted butter, softened
- 1/2 cup wild garlic leaves, finely chopped
- Salt (to taste)

Instructions:

1. **Mix Ingredients**: In a bowl, combine softened butter, wild garlic, and salt. Mix until well combined.
2. **Shape and Chill**: Transfer to parchment paper and roll into a log. Twist the ends to seal and refrigerate until firm.
3. **Use**: Slice and use on bread, vegetables, or as a topping for meats.

Rose Hip Jam

Ingredients:

- 2 cups rose hips, cleaned and chopped
- 1 cup water
- 1 cup sugar
- 1 tablespoon lemon juice

Instructions:

1. **Cook Rose Hips**: In a saucepan, combine rose hips and water. Bring to a boil, then simmer for 20-25 minutes until soft.
2. **Strain**: Strain the mixture through a fine mesh sieve to extract the juice.
3. **Make Jam**: In a clean pot, combine rose hip juice, sugar, and lemon juice. Cook over medium heat until thickened, about 15-20 minutes.
4. **Store**: Pour into sterilized jars and let cool before sealing.

Savory Mushroom Galette

Ingredients:

- 1 sheet pie crust (store-bought or homemade)
- 2 cups mushrooms, sliced (any variety)
- 1 cup ricotta cheese
- 1 tablespoon olive oil
- 1 clove garlic, minced
- Salt and pepper (to taste)
- Fresh herbs (like thyme or parsley), for garnish

Instructions:

1. **Preheat Oven**: Preheat the oven to 400°F (200°C).
2. **Sauté Mushrooms**: In a skillet, heat olive oil and sauté mushrooms and garlic until soft. Season with salt and pepper.
3. **Assemble Galette**: Roll out pie crust on a baking sheet. Spread ricotta cheese in the center, leaving a border. Top with sautéed mushrooms.
4. **Fold Edges**: Fold the edges of the crust over the filling, pleating as you go.
5. **Bake**: Bake for 25-30 minutes until golden. Garnish with fresh herbs before serving.

Enjoy these delightful recipes that highlight foraged and seasonal ingredients!

Wild Cherry Clafoutis

Ingredients:

- 2 cups wild cherries, pitted (or halved)
- 1 cup milk
- 3 large eggs
- 1/2 cup sugar
- 1 teaspoon vanilla extract
- 1/2 cup all-purpose flour
- Pinch of salt
- Butter (for greasing the pan)
- Powdered sugar (for serving, optional)

Instructions:

1. **Preheat Oven**: Preheat the oven to 350°F (175°C). Grease a pie dish or oven-safe skillet with butter.
2. **Prepare Cherries**: Spread the pitted wild cherries evenly in the prepared dish.
3. **Make Batter**: In a bowl, whisk together milk, eggs, sugar, vanilla extract, flour, and salt until smooth.
4. **Pour and Bake**: Pour the batter over the cherries. Bake for 35-40 minutes until puffed and golden.
5. **Cool and Serve**: Let cool slightly, then dust with powdered sugar if desired. Serve warm or at room temperature.

Dandelion Wine

Ingredients:

- 2 cups dandelion petals (fresh and clean, no green parts)
- 1 gallon water
- 2 lemons, juiced
- 2 oranges, juiced
- 3 cups sugar
- 1 packet wine yeast (or champagne yeast)

Instructions:

1. **Prepare Flowers**: In a large pot, bring water to a boil. Remove from heat and add dandelion petals, lemon juice, and orange juice. Let steep for 2-3 days, covered.
2. **Strain Mixture**: After steeping, strain the liquid through a fine mesh sieve or cheesecloth to remove the petals.
3. **Add Sugar and Yeast**: Return the liquid to the pot, add sugar, and stir until dissolved. Allow it to cool to room temperature, then add the wine yeast.
4. **Fermentation**: Transfer to a fermentation vessel, cover with a clean cloth, and let it ferment in a cool, dark place for about 1-2 weeks, until bubbling slows.
5. **Bottle and Age**: Siphon into bottles, leaving sediment behind. Seal and store in a cool, dark place for at least a month to age before tasting.

Enjoy these delightful, seasonal recipes!